Om Shri Ganeshaya Namah

To order additional copies of this book, contact:
Xlibris
844-714-8691
www.Xlibris.com
Orders@Xlibris.com

ISBN: Softcover   978-1-4415-6570-9
EBook   978-1-4771-7778-5

Print information available on the last page

Rev. date: 02/16/2022

# Birth of Ganesha

By Arvinda Khatri

*Mayureshwar*

Long ago, on Mount Kailash
in a beautiful palace lived the
mighty Lord Shiva and the
lovely Goddess Parvati.

2

Chintamani

Once while Goddess Parvati was going for her bath, she collected all the sandalwood from her body and with it created a strong and handsome boy.

4

Mahaganapati

Parvati recited a magic mantra and brought the boy to life. She told the boy to stand at the palace gate and said "Don't let anyone in while I bathe".

Siddhivinayak

Soon, Lord Shiva came to
the palace. The boy blocked
his way and said "You
can not go in". "This is my
own palace and I can go
anytime I want" said Lord
Shiva. But the boy wouldn't
let him in.

Lord Shiva became very angry
and pushed the boy out of
his way. The boy pulled out a
staff and attacked Lord Shiva.
During the fight the boy's
head was cut off.

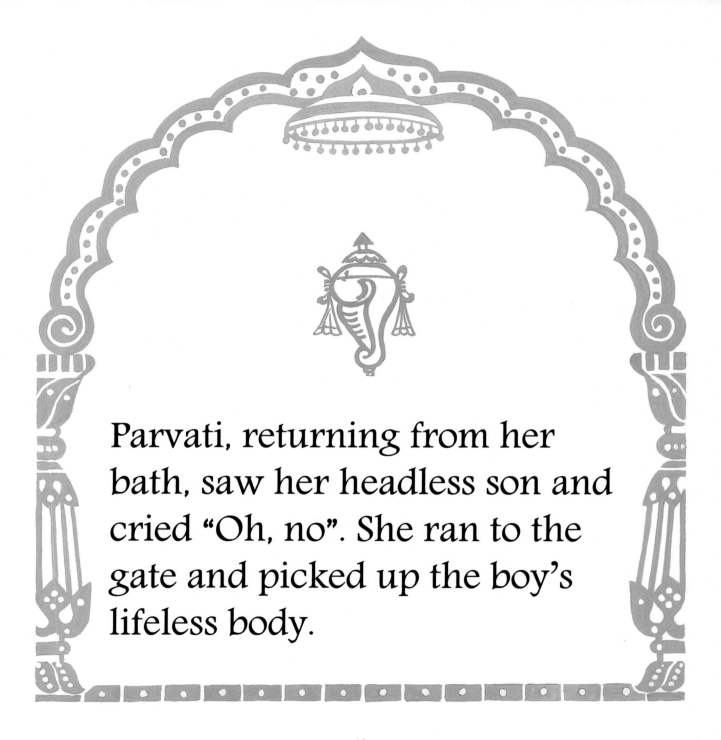

Parvati, returning from her bath, saw her headless son and cried "Oh, no". She ran to the gate and picked up the boy's lifeless body.

13

Seeing Parvati crying,
Lord Shiva promised to
replace the boy's head and
bring him back to life.

Lord Shiva asked the Gods to go
towards north and bring the head of the
first living being they would meet.

The Gods went north and searched the forest and found an elephant.

*Vighnahara*

The Gods brought the
elephant's head to Lord Shiva.

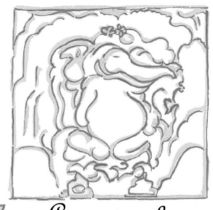

Girijatmak

Lord Shiva then placed the elephant head on the boy's lifeless body and brought him back to life.

Ballaleshwar

Goddess Parvati was overjoyed and hugged her elephant headed son.

22

23

Varad Vinayak

Lord Shiva named him Ganesh, the Lord of the people and they lived happily ever after.

25

## Ashta Vinayak

The eight forms of Ganesh are known as Ashta Vinayak. These eight shrines are located in Maharashtra, state of India. These are most important to Ganesh devotees.

## Mayureshwar – the most popular one is located at Morgaon

The form of Lord Ganesh named Mayureshwar is believed to have destroyed the demon Sindhu.

## Chintamani – located at Theur, close to Pune

Another form of Lord Ganesh is Chintamani, here he gets back the precious Chintamani jewel from the greedy Guna for saga Kapila.

## Mahaganapati – located at Ranjangaon

This form of Lord Ganesh is so called because here Lord Shiva worshipped Ganesh before fighting the demon, Tripuraasura.

## Siddhivinayak – located at Siddhatek

At this spot Lord Vishnu prayed to Ganesh before fighting with the demons Madhu and Kaitab, due to which he achieved success or Siddhi. This form of Ganesh has a right-sided-trunk.

## Vighnahara or Vighneshwara – located at Ojhar

Ganesh takes the form of Vighnahara & destroys a demon named Vighnaasura, who was created by Indra, the king of Gods.

## Girijatmak – located at Lenyadri

Girija is another name for Goddess Parvati. Parvati performs penance here to beget Ganapati as her son.

## Ballaleshwar – located in the town of Pali

Ballal, a boy who worshipped Vinayak was saved by Lord Ganesh when he was beaten up by local villagers.

## Varad Vinayak – located at Mahad, near Khopoli

This form of Ganesh is the giver of bounty and success. An oil lamp is permanently lighted here since 1892.

Printed in the United States
by Baker & Taylor Publisher Services